Writing Lessons from the Front: Book 3

Unlocking the mystery behind

Point of View

Angela Hunt

This lesson on point of view was originally published, in condensed form,

in *A Novel Idea*, published by Tyndale House Publishers.

Book 3 in the *Writing Lessons from the Front* Series

Hunt Haven
Press

Visit Angela Hunt's Web site at www.angelahuntbooks.com

ISBN: 0615841708
ISBN-13: 978-0615841700

"I have wanted you to see out of my eyes so many times."
— Elizabeth Berg, *The Pull of The Moon*

1 THE ONE AND ONLY CHAPTER

I don't know of any writing technique that ignites as many heated debates as point of view. One writer says that first person is cliché, another says it's practically required for genres like teen fiction and women's fiction. One critique group extols the use of "close third" or "subjective third" while another insists there is no such thing. One editor says that no one uses omniscient anymore; another says everyone uses omniscient at one point or another, they just don't realize they're using it.

I didn't write this book to create or undermine rules (because, after all, rules were made to be broken), but to help you understand what point of view is, how to tell when it's working and when it isn't, and how to unlock the secret power point of view brings to a writer's toolbox.

Point of View refers to the perspective from which a story is told, and, like ice cream, it comes in many flavors and varieties: first person, second person, third person. Third person limited, third person objective, third person subjective. Second person, the quirky but flavorful option. And the granddaddy of them all, omniscient.

Third Person Point of View

Can you guess what the most popular ice cream flavor is? Of all the ice cream companies surveyed in a poll taken by the International Ice Cream Association, 92 percent reported that vanilla was their best-selling flavor. Chocolate chip mint and cookies-and-cream tied for second place.

Third person point of view is like vanilla—perhaps the simplest, but also the most popular point of view choice. In this POV a narrator—the author—stands outside the character and relays information. Until he doesn't.

Example:

> When Mary woke up, she noticed it was raining.

Mary wouldn't refer to herself as "Mary," so someone else is relating this story—the author, a dispassionate and mostly invisible narrator. Think of him as a video camera. He starts at the edge of Mary's room—*When Mary woke up*—and moves almost immediately into her head, where he reports that she noticed the rain outside.

A third person POV can remain outside the character and report only on the observable facts, or it can move into the character's consciousness. It is, therefore, one of the most practical and versatile POV options.

If you have a paper towel tube handy (a toilet paper roll would work as well), bring it up to your eye and pretend you are looking through the third person camera. If you choose Mary as your POV character in a particular scene, you are *Mary's* camera, and except for that wee bit at the beginning when you were seeing her wake up, you must remain attached to Mary. Therefore you may only record things that Mary can see, hear, taste, touch, smell, feel, or think.

Why do we make an exception for those little phrases at the beginning of a scene? Because the writer has to give the reader some way of knowing whose POV we're venturing into. Without a phrase or some other clue, we could spend a minute or two floundering in confusion.

And that confusion would break the fictive dream, jostle our reader out of the story world, and remind him that a writer is at work. Such breaks are like the moment Toto pulled back the curtain to reveal that the great and powerful Oz was just a little balding man from Kansas. The reader doesn't want to see the writer doing his job, she wants to be swept along by the story.

Our goal as novelists is to create such a mesmerizing fictional world that the reader is unaware of passing time as she finds herself transported to a world with sights, smells, tastes, sensations, people and places of its own. To do that, writers should avoid words that are unclear in context, be careful not to indulge their penchant for purple prose, and find clear ways to let the reader know which camera she's looking through when she begins a new chapter.

Back to Mary: If we describe the scene only through Mary's eyes and thoughts we are using the point of view known as Third Person Limited—*limited* because the scene records the thoughts and experiences of one character only. Editors often recommend this point of view for beginning writers because it's relatively clear and consistent.

Most modern writers (and editors) prefer that POV be limited to one character per scene. Not per chapter; it's not so confining as that. The extra line of white space between scenes silently tells the reader that we have shifted in time, place, or perspective when a new scene begins.

The beauty of third person POV is its versatility. The camera may zoom in for closeups or remain at a distance. As the writer, you can choose to tell us a great deal about what Mary's thinking and feeling without having to italicize her thoughts or write "she thought." The reader intuitively understands that the camera is in her head, so why remind her? Respect your reader's intelligence enough to trust that they'll figure it out.

> When Mary woke up and looked out the window, she saw raindrops like tears upon the glass. She should have known the day would be as gray as her mood. Why did George have to leave her now?

The above paragraph, of course, reveals third person in all its glory. The camera started recording outside Mary, but immediately moved into her head. And here comes the beautiful, powerful part: as the narrator, you are so much in Mary's head that you use her vocabulary and her thoughts to relate the story. By doing so, you are accomplishing many things in a very few words. You are developing character, establishing mood, and providing narrative. So much work in so short a space!

Let me explain: Mary looked out the window and saw raindrops like *tears* upon the glass. The word *tears*, of course, came from me because I wrote that sentence, but I plucked it from my fictional Mary's thoughts. By using that word to describe the rain, what was I revealing about Mary's mood?

Her sadness, of course. Without having to use a narrator's voice to *tell* the reader that Mary was sad, without requiring the narrator to describe her broken heart, I allowed Mary's word choice to reveal her state of mind. That's *showing* versus telling. That's making every word work.

How would Mary have described the rain if she had awakened in a happy mood? Like *diamonds*? Like *jewels* or *crystals*? You bet. She might have even described the sky like "the grey of a soft blanket."

The example continues with thoughts that have come straight from Mary's head, but they've been translated into third person:

> She should have known the day would be as gray as her mood. Why did George have to leave her now?

Twenty years ago, the standard practice for writing interior monologue (thoughts) was to put the thought in italics and switch to first person. Writers believed this gave the writing a more intimate peek into a person's mind, and beaucoup writers handled thoughts this way.

But writing practices change, and today's readers want faster and smoother—we are a technological generation. We're accustomed to getting information instantly, we see words as images that play on the backs of our eyelids, and we want our reading experience to be as seamless as possible. So cut the unnecessary italics (and prevent your reader from squinting) and don't switch from third person to first. Why force your reader to change gears when he can simply keep reading what he already knows is coming from the character's consciousness?

So reserve italics for their proper use: emphasis, foreign phrases, and book titles. You don't need to employ them for a character's thoughts.

Third Person At a Distance

Sometimes, perhaps for reasons of prolonging suspense, you don't want your reader to know what the character is thinking. If you were writing in first person, in which the reader expects to be privy to all a character's pertinent thoughts and memories, you would be denying the reader what he had every right to know. In third person, however, you can simply withdraw the camera and switch from a "close up" to a shot a little farther back. We are still seeing things through the perspective of one character, but the tone is more like that of a detached observer.

Some writers call this detached POV "third person objective." In its purest form, the camera would never zoom in for the close up, never tell us what Mary was thinking, and would maintain an emotional distance from the character: think of it as the reporting of a fly on the wall.

> When Mary woke up, she saw rain pelting the window. She got out of bed and dressed quickly.

The above example is emotionally neutral. It is a simple recitation of facts: who, what, where. Mary woke up in her bedroom (we assume), then got dressed. No emotion-laden words to describe the rain, no interior monologue to relate what she's thinking and feeling.

This may be the preferred technique in some stories where a certain detachment serves the plot (perhaps a detective story?), but I'm not sure the payoff is worth sacrificing the bond that develops when the reader has full access to a character's consciousness (third person subjective.) Why not give yourself the best of both worlds and use "third person all-purpose?"

If anyone else enters the scene written in third person limited, we should *not* have access to that character's thoughts or feelings.

> Mary lowered her feet to the floor when Mother came into the room. "Why are you sleeping so late?" Mother asked, wondering why her daughter looked so pale. A bruise marked Mary's forehead.

Have you figured out why the above example is incorrect? With the phrase *wondering why her daughter looked so pale,* the camera has jumped into Mother's head and the writer is relating *Mom's* thoughts—and that's a problem because this is Mary's scene. Another problem exists in the next sentence: *A bruise marked Mary's forehead.* This is incorrect for a Mary POV scene because Mary can't see what's on her forehead, only Mother can.

But all is not lost. If you want to get in all of that information, go right ahead and include it. But do it from Mary's POV.

> Mary lowered her feet to the floor when Mother came into the room. "Why are you sleeping so late?" Mother asked. "You don't look well . . . and how did you get that bruise on your forehead?"

When a writer moves from one character's POV to another's in the same scene, this is often called "head-hopping" or "turning on a dime." Oddly enough, "head-hopping" is usually condemned in writer's circles while "turning on a dime" is accepted, but they are the same thing. And the writing will be clearer and less confusing for the reader if you don't jerk her around from one head to another.

(Note: like the use of interior monologue without italics, this is a style that has developed in the last twenty years. Many older writers—many of them best-selling novelists—have been happily head-hopping for years, and I doubt they'll change. Why should they, when they've enjoyed success writing the way they learned to write? But you should know that the preferred style these days is limited POV—one POV character per scene.)

When an editor points out that a writer is using more than one POV per scene, some writers will defend their technique by saying that they're simply using the omniscient voice. But head-hopping is not omniscient voice; omniscient is something else entirely. More on that later.

Take a look at these impromptu examples:

> Todd looked up as she came through the doorway. Mary hadn't changed at all. Despite the passing of fifteen years that had left him as worn out as a slipper than had been chewed on and dragged through the mud, Mary looked as young and carefree as she had at graduation.
>
> He subconsciously flexed his jaw and straightened his spine. Maybe she'd remember him.

See the problem? Common little words—like *subconsciously*—can creep into our prose when we're writing in the flow, but if we stop and think about it, we realize that we can't be in Todd's consciousness while something subconscious is going on. Subconscious actions take place below a person's consciousness, so that POV camera is all over the place in that example.

Why not just delete the word *subconsciously*? Makes things a lot easier for you and your reader.

Here's another situation to consider:

> Jenna lowered her head into her hands and wept silently. Tomorrow had to be better. Her situation had to improve. Because she couldn't handle another day like today.
>
> Little did she know what life had to offer in the next twenty-four hours.

Ah—that last sentence did *not* come from Jenna's head. It's the clear voice of a narrator, and how can it belong in a book that is written in third person?

Some writers will defend a sentence like this, calling it the literary equivalent of a camera pulling away at the end of a scene. I see their logic, but whenever I'm reading a book and come across something like this, it always jars me. But, to be fair, writers make the most critical readers. So while this does make me lift a brow, it probably wouldn't bother the average reader.

I wouldn't make a habit of ending a scene in a narrator's voice, but I also wouldn't mind the occasional use of an omniscient exit line. After all, we often begin scenes with omniscient entrance lines, so fair is fair.

So there you have it: third person, the vanilla ice cream of the literary world. Everyone loves it, it is amazingly versatile, and it works in practically any genre. You can't go wrong with third person, but you might find a better option with another POV choice.

First Person Point of View

If third person is vanilla ice cream, first person is chocolate mint chip. People who love it adore it, and some genres almost require it. It is de rigueur in most novels for teenage girls (*Twilight*, *The Hunger Games*, *Matched*, *The Fault in Our Stars*, just to name a few recent titles) and chick lit, and easily accepted in women's fiction.

First person allows you to tell the story in the character's own voice, but without the distance you find when you relate those feelings in third person. You can cover the same emotional territory in first person as in third, but using "I" instead of "she" imparts a greater emotional intimacy.

Let's listen to Mary when the camera begins the story in her head and *stays* in her head:

> When I woke up I noticed it was raining. Rivulets streaked the windowpanes like tears, and the sky was as gray as my mood. Why did George have to leave me now?

Compare that to our third person version:

> When Mary woke up and looked out the window, she saw raindrops like tears upon the glass. She should have known the day would be as gray as her mood. Why did George have to leave her now?

Do you see the difference?

The only drawback to using first person is that in its purest form, using first person requires that the *entire book* be written in first person. So if I were writing in Mary's first person POV and I wanted to include a scene where George confesses himself to Father Tom, I couldn't include it in the novel because Mary wasn't present at the confessional.

I could, of course, have George go to Mary later and tell her about what happened when he went to confession. Or I could have Father Tom break the sanctity of the confessional and tell Mary what George said—and those are valid options, especially if this is the only scene I need that can't be covered by Mary in her first person POV.

Like millions of other girls and women, I read the Twilight series and was swept into another world populated by benign vampires and teenage love. But, like millions of other girls and women, I was always a little mystified as to what Edward saw in awkward, fumbling Bella. I accepted his declarations of love as true, but something inside me kept wondering why Bella had captured his heart . . .

Then Stephenie Meyer began writing *Midnight Sun*. It was the same story of *Twilight*—Edward and Bella meet for the first time at Forks High School—but all the scenes were from Edward's point of view. (Meyer never finished the book, by the way, but copies of the partial manuscript are available online.)

You might think a novel that covers the same territory would be dull and repetitive, but I found it fascinating and so did thousands of other readers. It was the same story, yes, but this time we saw events through Edward's perspective. We learned more of his personal history, and—finally!—we saw what attracted him to Bella. He watched her, he saw that she had come to Forks to help out her mother, he saw that she was sensitive and an old soul . . . she was *selfless*.

And after reading all that, I found myself wishing that Meyer had written *Twilight* in third person, so we could get scenes from Edward *and* Bella. We could have seen events from both perspectives in one book, and to my way of thinking, the characterization would have gone even deeper.

But who am I to argue with success of Myer's books? My wish will remain just that—a whimsical thought. But I think this example does illustrate how first person works—in its purest form, first person POV creates the strongest bond possible between reader and protagonist. But its principal drawback is that it doesn't allow the reader to bond as deeply with the other characters because we will never see things from their point of view.

What About Mixed POV?

Some writers—myself included—have compromised with the stringent use of first-person-only in a book. I'm sure mixed POV has existed in many books, but I first noticed it in the novels of Diana Gabaldon. Her Outlander series features a female physician, Claire, who travels back through time and falls in love with Jaime, an eighteenth-century Scotsman. All of Claire's scenes are written in first person—lots of intimacy—and everyone else'sscenes (and the books feature a huge cast of characters) are written in third person POV.

Did this use of mixed point of view lessen my enjoyment of Gabaldon's story? Not in the least. Did it jar me from the fictive dream? Not a bit.

So I began to used mixed POV myself. I used it in *The Immortal,*

The Novelist, and in *The Note*. I've probably used it in other books I can't remember, but I've used it often enough to know that mixed POV is not a big deal if done consistently.

If you're going to mix POV, then you should choose a character, assign him a POV, and stick to it. Don't write Missy Shaw in first person in chapter one and in third person in chapter four. Stick to your pattern throughout the book or you're bound to confuse your reader.

I recently read a novel that violated this principle—and reading the book drove me crazy. I never felt connected with the protagonist and I was never sure who I was reading about until well into each scene. I'm not sure what the writer was doing— maybe trying to be inventive?—but his disjointed approach didn't work for me. Others might call it genius, but for me it's not about how creative and unusual the writing is. I care first and foremost about the strength of the story, and this particular story was so fragmented that I nearly stopped caring about the characters.

Second Person Point of View

Second Person Point of View is the bubble gum flavor of ice cream. It's delicious, but a bit annoying because you have to work on holding the bubble gum in your mouth while trying to swallow the ice cream and cone. You end up asking yourself if the flavor was worth the effort.

Here's our example with Mary:

> You woke up to rain this morning. Water streaked your windowpanes like tears, and your heart felt as gray as the sky outside. Why did George have to get all freaky and leave you now? Because he was a jerk, that's why. Or maybe he just didn't like you.

I've never written in second person, but a friend of mine has, so it's not as rare as you might think. It's still a bit odd, and whether or not your reader will bond with the protagonist probably depends upon whether your reader accepts this quirky POV. I've had Amazon readers remark that they put a book down because they didn't like my (occasional) novels in present tense, so I have to wonder how many readers would put up with something as unusual as second person POV. I would end up asking myself if the flavor was worth the effort?

Omniscient POV

Omniscient POV is often called the "God view" because the unseen narrator sees and knows all—or as much as the writer wants him to know:

> In the house on Forty-second Street, at six-fifteen in the morning, Mary Jones opened her eyes and thought the raindrops on her window looked like tears. Why had George chosen to leave her now? He had his reasons, of course, none of which were known to Mary. But in his heart of hearts, he knew he would never be the man she needed. Or wanted. Because she could never accept his secret. And secrets, as the sages say, have a way of bubbling to the surface.

Did you notice the swift movement of the POV camera? It is swooping everywhere. First it hovers outside Mary Jones's house, then it moves into her bedroom and into her head, where it notes that she thought the raindrops looked like tears. The omniscient narrator then relates her silent thought: why had George chosen to leave her now?

The camera/narrator then flies outside of Mary's head and dives into George's, because the narrator knows about George's reasons and knows that Mary doesn't know what George was really thinking.

But the narrator knows. He knows that George feels inferior, and that he will never be the kind of man Mary needs or wants. The narrator also knows that George has a secret . . . and we assume that the narrator knows what the secret is.

Then the narrator pulls away from George and speaks directly to the reader. *Secrets, as the sages say, have a way of bubbling to the surface.*

Can't you just hear the snide smile in his voice? That last line isn't from Mary's head or George's; it's the narrator enticing us with a teasing promise of secrets and suspense to come.

An omniscient narrator has a distinct voice. A writer who merely head-hops within a scene, jumping from head to head, is not writing in omniscient, he's simply leap-frogging from character to character.

The omniscient point of view, according to my favorite handbook to literature, is:

> A term used to describe the point of view in a work of fiction in which the author is capable of knowing, seeing, and telling whatever he or she wishes in the story, and exercises this freedom at will. It is characterized by freedom in shifting from the exterior world to the inner selves of a number of characters and by a freedom in movement in both time and place; but to an even **greater extent it is characterized by the freedom of the author to comment upon the meaning of actions and to state the thematic intentions of the story whenever and wherever the author desires.**[1] (Emphasis added.)

Omniscient was a common POV in the time of Dickens, who gave us this possibly-the-most-famous-of-all-omniscient-openings:

> It was the best of times, it was the worst of times, it was the age of wisdom, it was the age of foolishness, it was the epoch of belief, it was the epoch of incredulity, it was the season of Light, it was the season of Darkness, it was the spring of hope, it was the winter of despair, we had everything before us, we had nothing before us, we were all going direct to Heaven, we were all going direct the other way—in short, the period was so far like the present period, that some of its noisiest authorities insisted on its being received, for good or for evil, in the superlative degree of comparison only. [2]

So begins Charles Dickens' tale of two look-alikes in two cities, a sweeping story that spans two countries and two men's hearts. His omniscient voice is that of an orator: big, bold, and poetic. He narrates more gently when he is writing scenes, but at the ending, when his unlikely and self-sacrificing hero is about to mount the steps to the guillotine, he resumes his poetic tone once more:

> They said of him, about the city that night, that it was the peacefullest man's face ever beheld there. Many added that he looked sublime and prophetic.[3]

This is the narrator's voice; he is telling us about a scene as though he were a reporter gathering impressions and quotes from people in the crowd.

One of my favorite omniscient novels is William Goldman's *The Princess Bride*. After opening the book you'll likely have to wade through several letters, forewords, and acknowledgements to even find the beginning of this novel, but it's worth the search:

> The year that Buttercup was born, the most beautiful woman in the world was a French scullery maid named Annette. Annette worked in Paris for the Duke and Duchess de Guiche, and it did not escape the Duke's notice that someone extraordinary was polishing the pewter. The Duke's notice did not escape the notice of the Duchess either, who was not very beautiful and not very rich, but plenty smart. The Duchess set about studying Annette and shortly found her adversary's tragic flaw.
> Chocolate.[4]

And so begins the tale of Buttercup and Wesley, but the omniscient narrator feels free to tell us about Annette and her employers, his agent, his wife, and many other adventures as he lets the tale unwind. Furthermore, he tells a historic tale in modern lingo, and his deliciously droll voice adds charm that would be lost if William Goldman had chosen to tell the story in straight third or even first person. Unless, perhaps, Goldman had decided to turn Wesley into a wry commentator on modern society.

Margaret Mitchell uses an omniscient point of view in *Gone with the Wind,* telling us right away that

> Scarlett O'Hara was not beautiful, but men seldom realized it when caught by her charm as the Tarleton twins were. In her face were too sharply blended the delicate features of her mother, a Coast aristocrat of French descent, and the heavy ones of her florid Irish father. But it was an arresting face, pointed of chin, square of jaw.[5]

Disclaimer: I should tell you that *Gone with the Wind* is one of my favorite books. I first read it in the fifth grade, and have read it many times since. I have sections memorized. I used to read it aloud, playing the parts of Scarlett and Rhett. I learned how to flirt from reading this book.

But it wasn't until many years later that I realized the power of point of view as revealed in *GWTW*.

Margaret Mitchell uses omniscient point of view to open the book and many chapters and scenes, especially when reporting on news of the war—news and details that Scarlett wouldn't have known.

But after Mitchell is finished with her reporting, she usually dives immediately into Scarlett's head and remains there for the rest of the scene. In fact, we are in Scarlett's head 99 percent of the time. Every once in a while, when Scarlett is not present, Mitchell will dip into Melanie's head, Wade Hampton's, or continue with her narrative, but I don't think she ever allows us access to Rhett Butler's or Ashley's thoughts. We have only their words to tell us what they are thinking, and neither of those two men want Scarlett to know the truth. Ashley doesn't want Scarlett to know his love is a mixture of lust and admiration, and Rhett doesn't want Scarlett to know he loves her passionately—because she'd use his love against him if she knew. So he teases her and lies to her and makes sly jests. We never know whether or not take him seriously, and neither does Scarlett.

And that is why the book is far, far better than the movie.

In the classic film, Rhett Butler frequently expresses his love for Scarlett. And because the unblinking camera is a neutral observer, movie watchers have no reason to doubt his sincerity. He *behaves* like he loves Scarlett, so why should we doubt him?

But in the book, every time Rhett expresses his love for Scarlett, we have access to her thoughts so we know she doesn't believe him. She dismisses him so completely—he's trying to get something from her, he's only saying that to make her angry, he's already told her he's not a marrying man—that we dismiss him, too.

And on that foggy night after Melanie's death, as Scarlett walks back to her lonely mansion in Atlanta, she has the mother of all epiphanies—why, Rhett really *does* love her! He sacrificed for her, and spoiled her, and risked his life for her because his love was *real*. And all of his posturing and protesting and pretending that he didn't care for her was only an act to protect his vulnerable heart.

Scarlett realizes that she has been a fool, so she runs home to Rhett, only to find that the years of her indifference and selfishness have worn out his love. He's too exhausted and broken to care anymore.

But Scarlett is forever confident—she *will* win him back. Because she refuses to be defeated. And tomorrow *is* another day.

Do you see the difference POV makes? By keeping the reader out of Rhett Butler's head, Margaret Mitchell persuaded us that Scarlett was right—Rhett didn't love her. Perhaps, as he intimated, he wanted her the way a collector wants a pretty doll to set on a shelf.

So Scarlett's epiphany results in a shock of understanding for the reader, too.

In the movie, however, we believe Rhett when he goes around saying, "I love ya, Scarlett," so the epiphany is not nearly as powerful as it is in the book.

Your choices regarding point of view—which POV to use, and whose POV to reveal—can make a tremendous impact on your story.

Which POV to Use?

Before deciding upon a point of view, check out other examples in your genre. Chick Lit, for one example, is usually written in first person, present tense. A lot of young adult novels use first person. Magical realism (*Like Water for Chocolate, Perfume*) almost always calls for omniscient point of view. You can certainly ignore these guidelines, but you do so at your own risk. Editors and readers may prefer books that abide by the traditional blueprint for the genre.

Third person works well for stories with many characters. Each character will have his own perspective, and readers can learn about their goals (which may conflict with your protagonist's) through POV character's thoughts, actions, and dialogue.

One word of warning here: if there's one thing I've learned from my book club, it's this: the more point of view characters you use, the more you will dilute the bond between your reader and your characters. When we read a book with only one POV character, we bond deeply with that character. That bond is weakened, however, when we introduce someone else—it literally becomes a case of divided loyalties. On and on it goes, until the reader gets worn out by trying to keep up with the cast of POV characters.

I try to limit the number of point of view characters to five or less. Notice I didn't limit the *number of characters*—you will need as many as it takes to tell the story—but the number of characters *through whom* you tell the story.

(Practical hint: I always create a timeline that looks like an Excel chart. The rows are filled in with scene details, and the columns give me spaces to jot down POV character/date and time/weather/mood/events of the scene/etc. I assign each POV character a certain color, so with a glance at my chart I can tell if I'm using a minor character too often, forgetting a major character for too long, or using a POV character so rarely that I should eliminate his POV altogether. You may find this tip useful—or the thought of constructing an Excel chart may give you hives. In that case, ignore this paragraph and read on.)

Third Person can also be quite intimate if you "zoom in" as we did in the example with Mary. It may not be quite as intimate as first person, but it can come pretty close. Furthermore, you can use this "zoom" feature with any POV character, not just the protagonist, as you would be if you were writing in the pure first person form.

Third person is also useful if you're writing a mystery or thriller and you don't want to reveal clues to the reader too soon. If you're writing in First Person, the reader expects to have complete access to the protagonist's thoughts, feelings, and memories. In Third Person, it's permissible to withhold certain thoughts, feelings, and memories if it serves your plot. In Sherlock Holmes novels, for instance, the story is told not by Holmes, but by Watson . . . because Sir Arthur Conan Doyle didn't want the reader to be privy to Holmes' deductive reasoning until the unmasking of the criminal. It's much more fun to leave the reader in suspense until the detective explains everything.

First Person works well for stories where the main character needs to give readers full access to angst. Readers live with the main character throughout the story and have immediate access to the protagonist's thoughts and feelings. Make sure, however, that you have created a *likeable* protagonist. Readers won't want to spend an entire book in the head of someone they despise.

One tendency to guard against in First Person POV is the temptation to get caught up in stream-of-consciousness writing (recording every thought that pops into a character's head), that the pace becomes sluggish and the story becomes crowded with ruminations that do nothing to advance plot or deepen character. If paragraphs do not move story events forward or shine a light on some unrevealed aspect of your protagonist, highlight and hit the delete key.

(Really, I can think of only two occasions when you should let yourself yield to a stream-of-consciousness passage: when a character is drunk, suffering from a high fever, or both. If any of those situations apply, go for it.)

If you want to use omniscient point of view, you'll need a good reason for doing so. This POV is not as popular today as it was generations ago, but it occasionally pops up in best-sellers (though I just grabbed a handful of recent best-sellers from my bookshelf and couldn't find an omniscient POV among them).

Probably the most important consideration in deciding upon which POV to use is the story itself. What do you want to reveal? What do you want to hide?

In my book *The Note*, I knew that my protagonist, Peyton MacGruder, had once tried to kill herself while pregnant. She had subsequently spent time and gave birth in a mental hospital. Her father, acting as her legal guardian while she was incapacitated, signed papers surrendering her baby to an adoption agency, and the child was placed with a family.

I knew these things by the time I started my second draft, but I didn't want my reader to know them until the end of the book. So which POV did I choose?

Third person. If I'd used first person, my reader would have expected to have full access to my character's thoughts and memories. And since Peyton wouldn't have been able to look at a baby without shivering at the memory of the infant taken from her, I would have had a hard time justifying my slamming the door on her memories until the end of the book.

On the other hand, in my novel *The Pearl*, I knew I would be writing about a mother who lost her precious five-year-old son in a freak accident. She would then be approached by an organized group who would offer to clone the son she'd lost. I knew my readers would find this not only troubling, but highly unbelievable, so I wanted to make them feel every emotion, think every thought, weigh every option, and understand exactly why my protagonist would agree to cloning. I needed them to have full access to her angst, so I chose to write her scenes in first person POV.

You shouldn't just flip a coin when deciding your point of view—consider the genre, the story, and whether or not your protagonist will be in every scene. Those are the key considerations.

Special Situations

I was critiquing manuscripts at a writers' conference when a woman came up with her story. I asked about the protagonist, and she said he was a child.

"So this is a children's book?" I asked.

"Oh, no. It's an adult book. It's about these children who find a dead body. It's based on something that happened in my childhood."

I took her manuscript and skimmed the first few paragraphs. "How old is this child?"

"About seven."

I shook my head. "I see a problem here. You've got this seven-year-old using words only an adult would know. You've said he's a kid, but he's talking like a grown-up."

She frowned. "Then how am I supposed to write this story?"

She had inadvertently stumbled across a problem related to point of view: if your point of view character is a child, then nearly all the words you use in that scene *should be the words of a child*. Everything in the scene ostensibly comes from his head, so you'll have to use a child's vocabulary to write the scene. If you do it well, you'll create a very convincing character.

The same principle applies if you're writing a scene in the point of view of a recent immigrant . . . a highly educated doctor . . . a

Southern socialite . . . or an overachieving lawyer.

All of us have certain phrases we use because we picked them up in our profession, our background, or from our region. Make sure the scenes featuring particular characters feature lingo and language they would use and nothing that they wouldn't.

By the way—if you don't want to restrict your adult book featuring children to a child's vocabulary, consider Harper Lee's *To Kill a Mockingbird*.

> When he was nearly thirteen, my brother Jem got his arm badly broken at the elbow. When it healed, and Jem's fears of never being able to play football were assuaged, he was seldom self-conscious about his injury. . . .
>
> When enough years had gone by to enable us to look back on them, we sometimes discussed the events leading to his accident. I maintain that the Ewells started it all, but Jem, who was four years my senior, said it started long before that. He said it began the summer Dill came to us, when Dill first gave us the idea of making Boo Radley come out.[6]

Scout tells the story of what happened to her as a young girl, but she tells the story as an adult looking back. Harper Lee was free to use a full adult's vocabulary, understanding, and emotions. This technique—often called an *envelope story* because the ending wraps back around to the beginning—opens with an adult's voice and transports the reader back to a particular time in the narrator's youth. It usually returns to the adult's voice at the ending, sealing the "envelope." The technique is probably the best and most popular way to tell an adult story about something that happened to a child.

While I was writing *Journey*, a novel set in ancient Egypt, I noticed that several of the ancient pharaohs had blind harpists among the court musicians. So I decided to write a blind harpist into my book, and I made her the love interest of two rival brothers.

Well—easier said than done. Almost immediately I realized that I faced a challenge—in every scene from the harpist's point of view, I could not refer to anything visual because she couldn't see it. I would have to describe places and people only by using sounds, smells, sensations, tastes, and feelings.

> Jendayi followed her handmaid through the palace halls and tried to deny the sour feeling in the pit of her stomach. She was glad Pharaoh would not be summoning her to play again tonight, for nothing but loneliness, longing, and pain could pour from her harp now.
>
> She heard Akil's shuffling steps behind her and lowered her head, knowing he would be angry if he read her feelings on her face . . .
>
> Life itself haunted her, for living seemed an exercise she often heard about but would never really experience. She ate, slept, drank, and played in the lonely blackness of the blind; every day looked like every night. Each time she rose from her bed she slipped into a tunic that felt like the one she had worn the day before; the sounds that rose and fell around her were the same sounds that had kept her company since the days of her childhood. The people who moved along the fringes of her world raised their voices when speaking as if she were deaf, or they were quick to assume that because she did not make eye contact with them, they could not make contact with her . . .[7]

Notice all the sensual details *other* than images? When once sense is disallowed, you have to make the most of the others.

If you find yourself faced with a point of view challenge in your novel, don't worry—just close your eyes, slip into the skin of that POV character, and write the story as he would tell it.

If you have the opportunity, you should read novelist Mark Haddon's *The Curious Incident of the Dog in the Night-Time*. This novel features an autistic boy as the protagonist and first person point of view character. Haddon does a wonderful job of writing in the voice of an autistic British boy. Not only is it a good story, it's a beautiful example of point of view handled well.

Here's the first paragraph:

It was 7 minutes after midnight. The dog was lying on the grass in the middle of the lawn in front of Mrs. Shears's house. Its eyes were closed. It looked as if it was running on its side, the way dogs run when they think they are chasing a cat in a dream. But the dog was not running or asleep. The dog was dead. There was a garden fork sticking out of the dog. The points of the fork must have gone all the way through the dog and into the ground because the fork had not fallen over. I decided that the dog was probably killed with the fork because I could not see any other wounds in the dog and I do not think you would stick a garden fork into a dog after it had died for some other reason like cancer, for example, or a road accident. But I could not be certain about this.[8]

Isn't that beautiful writing? Notice that Haddon uses no contractions, a feature of colloquial language that would be foreign to this child, and the boy speaks in complete, factual sentences. Already we understand that we are inside the mind of a very unique person.

The Foolproof Way to Determine the Best POV

Still uncertain about which point of view you should use in your novel? Don't let uncertainty stop you, but start writing. Write a scene in first person, if that's a viable option, and read it aloud. Then write it in third person and read aloud. Finally, try writing it in omniscient and read it aloud.

Which scene was easiest to write? In which did the story seem to flow most naturally? Which scene sounded best when you read it aloud?

Which point of view suits your story best? If you've chosen first person and you are planning to include important scenes where your protagonist will not be present, can you have the events of that scene recounted later? Or can you choose another character to write in first or third person and use them, in that particular POV, throughout the novel?

Most important, which scene appeals to you most? Can you write the entire story in that point of view?

More than once I have finished an entire novel in one point of view, then turned around and changed it to something else. You'll know when you hit upon the point of view that works best.

Point of view can be tricky until you get used to practicing it, then it will come more naturally. As you grow more relaxed with the technique and learn to submerge yourself into your charcters' thoughts and feelings, point of view will become a powerful weapon in your writer's arsenal.

Why write:

Joe Smith propped his foot on the lower bleacher and watched his son on the field. He smiled as happiness rose within him, bringing tears to his eyes and embarrassing him in front of his friend, Tom Harris. Tom glanced his way, then handed him a handkerchief, keeping his blue eyes on the baseball diamond.

"Yeah," Tom said, obviously understanding the emotion that had moved Joe and the resulting embarrassment. "I know."

When you could write:

Joe Smith propped his foot on the lower bleacher and watched his son through foolish tears.

Tom glanced his way, then handed him a handkerchief. "Yeah." He kept his blue gaze on the diamond. "I know."

Go find an empty paper towel roll. Then sit at your computer and write something wonderful.

Look for another *Lesson from the Writing Front* soon.

ABOUT THE AUTHOR

Angela Hunt writes for readers who have learned to expect the unexpected from this versatile writer. With over four million copies of her books sold worldwide, she is the best-selling author of more than 120 works ranging from picture books (*The Tale of Three Trees*) to novels and nonfiction.

Now that her two children have reached their twenties, Angie and her husband live in Florida with Very Big Dogs (a direct result of watching *Turner and Hooch* too many times). This affinity for mastiffs has not been without its rewards—one of their dogs was featured on *Live with Regis and Kelly* as the second-largest canine in America. Their dog received this dubious honor after an all-expenses-paid trip to Manhattan for the dog and the Hunts, complete with VIP air travel and a stretch limo in which they toured New York City. Afterward, the dog gave out pawtographs at the airport.

Angela admits to being fascinated by animals, medicine, unexplained phenomena, and "just about everything." Books, she says, have always shaped her life— in the fifth grade she learned how to flirt from reading *Gone with the Wind*.

Her books have won the coveted Christy Award, several Angel Awards from Excellence in Media, and the Gold and Silver Medallions from *Foreword Magazine*'s Book of the Year Award. In 2007, her novel *The Note* was featured as a Christmas movie on the Hallmark channel. She recently completed her doctorate in biblical literature and is now finishing her doctorate in Theology.

When she's not home writing, Angie often travels to teach writing workshops at schools and writers' conferences. And to talk about her dogs, of course. Readers may visit her web site at www.angelahuntbooks.com.

Selected Books by Angela Hunt

The Offering
The Fine Art of Insincerity
Five Miles South of Peculiar
The Face
Let Darkness Come
The Elevator
The Novelist
The Awakening
The Truth Teller
Unspoken
Uncharted
The Justice
The Canopy
The Immortal
Doesn't She Look Natural?
She Always Wore Red
She's In a Better Place
The Pearl
The Note
The Debt
Then Comes Marriage
The Shadow Women
Dreamers
Brothers
Journey
Roanoke
Jamestown
Hartford
Rehoboth
Charles Towne
The Proposal
The Silver Sword
The Golden Cross
The Velvet Shadow
The Emerald Isle

ENDNOTES

[1]C. Hugh Holman, *A Handbook to Literature* (Indianapolis: Bobbs-Merrill Educational Publishing, 1980), p. 308.

[2]Charles Dickens*, A Tale of Two Cities* (New York: Nelson Doubleday, Inc.), p. 9.

[3] Dickens, *op.cit.*, p. 350.

[4]William Goldman, The Princess Bride (New York: Harcourt, 2007).

[5] Margaret Mitchell, *Gone With the Wind* (New York: the Macmillan Company, 1936), p. 1.

[6]Harper Lee, *To Kill a Mockingbird* (New York: Harper, 2010).

[7]Angela Hunt, *Journey* (New York: Steeple Hill, 2009).

[8] Mark Haddon, *The Curious Incident of the Dog in the Night Time* (New York: Vintage, 2004).

3738173R00018

Made in the USA
San Bernardino, CA
17 August 2013